NEVER MIND
THE JAMBOS

NEVER MIND THE JAMBOS

The Ultimate HEARTS FC

QUIZ BOOK

JOHN McBURNIE

The History Press

First published 2014

The History Press
The Mill, Brimscombe Port
Stroud, Gloucestershire, GL5 2QG
www.thehistorypress.co.uk

Reprinted 2016, 2017

© John McBurnie, 2014

The right of John McBurnie to be identified as the Author
of this work has been asserted in accordance with the
Copyright, Designs and Patents Act 1988.

British Library Cataloguing in Publication Data.
A catalogue record for this book is available from the British Library.

ISBN 978 0 7524 9879 9

Typesetting and origination by The History Press
Printed in Great Britain

Contents

Foreword
by Jim Jefferies

(Hearts player (and captain) 1969–1981, manager 1995–2000 and 2010–2011)

Having had strong connections with the Jambos as a supporter, player and the great privilege of managing the club for two spells, it goes without saying that when John McBurnie asked me to write this foreword, I was delighted to accept – especially as John had, on a number of occasions, invited me to the Manchester Hearts Supporters Club's annual Player of the Year dinner dance.

I am sure this quiz book should prove to be very popular with a wide range of ages among Hearts supporters, as it poses some very interesting questions relating to a long period in the club's history.

John is one of the most dedicated supporters of the club I know and it is obvious he has put a lot of effort into this quiz book.

I'm sure you will have a lot of fun and some head scratching – as I did.

Hope you enjoy it!

Introduction

If you ever listened to the rhythmical tones of James Alexander Gordon reading out the football results on BBC Radio 5 Live's *Sports Report* on a Saturday, you'll know exactly which club has the most romantic name in football. 'Heart of Midlothian 5, (insert any other team here) 0.' OK, it doesn't happen very often, but we're allowed to dream aren't we?

The very sound of the name conjures up one of Sir Walter Scott's most celebrated novels, the iconic image built into the cobbles on Edinburgh's Royal Mile, or simply arouses the fascination of the curious.

Having lived and worked south of the border for nearly forty years, I've met countless football fans who have adopted the famous 'Boys in Maroon' as their favoured Scottish team – and, on my weekly journey north, I've driven many of them to Tynecastle for an initial pilgrimage which has, in many cases, turned into a regular trip.

If you are one of those devotees who pull on a maroon and white scarf every weekend, or if you've just taken a shine to the number one team in Scotland's capital city, then this is the book for you. It's perfect for testing your fellow travellers on those long away trips, tormenting your football-mad mates in the pub or as a stocking-filler for a Junior Jambo.

There are questions here for everyone, from the never-miss-a-match diehard to the casual fan – tough ones to test your knowledge of the club's history, easy ones about recent matches and players, cryptic ones to get your brain cells working and infuriating ones that will nag you all the way to Pittodrie.

Which player was signed from where? Who scored the winner in the cup final? Where have our European adventures taken us? All the big events are in here.

Each round contains eleven questions, just like the number of players in our team, though a few questions carry a supplementary extra. (Well, it's a squad game nowadays, isn't it?)

Good luck, happy quizzing …
'Follow the Hearts and you can't go wrong.'

John McBurnie, 2014

The Romanov Years

It was madcap, it was glorious, it was sometimes cringeworthy and, ultimately, it was heartbreaking. In the rollercoaster history of Heart of Midlothian Football Club, surely no period has been more eventful than the Romanov Era.

When the Lithuania-based Russian banker, Vladimir Romanov, bought control of Hearts in 2005, it was a club in crisis. He was hailed as the saviour who stopped the rot. Tynecastle fans then witnessed eight bizarre years punctuated by mad Romanov rants, victory parades, bizarre publicity stunts, a revolving door in the manager's office, player revolt, transfer embargoes, appeals to supporters for life-saving cash injections and, finally, financial meltdown. By the time Romanov relinquished control in the summer of 2013, the club had turned full circle, was once more in crisis, and in the hands of the administrators.

Just to get you going, the first round of questions is a jog through some of the outstanding events of these unforgettable Romanov years.

1 Who was Hearts manager when Vladimir Romanov gained overall control of the club?

2   In 2011, where did Vladimir Romanov go for a swim to help raise funds for a new lifeboat station?

3   How many different managers, including caretakers, took charge of the first team during the Romanov era?

4   Who was 'Fireworks Phil'?

5   Who did Vladimir Romanov persistently refer to as 'monkeys' in his regular rants?

6   During pre-season training in 2007, Vladimir Romanov staged a boxing bout in which he went up against which player?

7   Which club did Hearts defeat during their only entry to the Champions League qualifying rounds?

8   Who were the 'Riccarton Three'?

9   After months of reports that Romanov was interfering with team affairs, it was finally confirmed that he had picked the team for a match in February 2007. Who were the opponents on that occasion?

10 During season 2011–12, as cash flow problems beset the club and players found they were not being paid on time, how did midfield star Ian Black earn extra cash to tide him over?

11 Which company held security over Tynecastle when Hearts went into administration as a result of Romanov's mismanagement of the club?

In the Beginning

OK, you only needed a short-term memory for the first round. Now the serious stuff starts. If you know your history, you'll know all about how, when and where Edinburgh's number one football club began its existence, and if you have ever worn a maroon and white scarf, you should be familiar with all the club's important landmarks. If you don't get more than half of these right, you need to read up on your Hearts history.

1 Which pub did the newly formed Heart of Midlothian FC use as its headquarters?

2 Who were Hearts' first opponents in the Scottish Cup?

3 What colour was Hearts' first playing kit?

4 What was the first trophy won by Hearts?

5 Bobby Walker, possibly Hearts' most celebrated player, joined the club as a 17 year old in 1896. From which club was he signed?

6 Hearts made their first foray into England in January 1881. Which two English clubs did they play against on that trip?

7 Hearts' biggest recorded victory was achieved in the Edinburgh FA Cup in 1880. Who were the opponents and what was the result?

8 Why were Hearts suspended by the SFA in 1884?

9 Who did Hearts play in their first league match after the Scottish League was formed in 1890?

10 In which season did Hearts win their first Scottish League title?

11 As the top English clubs began to poach players from Hearts' successful side in the early days of the 1900s, Tynecastle star Albert Buick was transferred down south and subsequently lured six other players to join him. Which English club did they all join?

Round

3

Goals, Goals, Goals

Well, there's no better sight in football, is there? Seeing the ball hit the back of the net – as long as it's in the other team's net!

We've spent hours on away trips remembering some of our favourite Hearts goals in seasons past. In this section, we recall famous goals, spectacular goals, vital goals, bizarre goals and barrowloads of goals. What do you remember about the following?

1　Which Hearts player scored Scotland's first-ever goal in a World Cup finals tournament?

2　Against which opponents did Donald Ford score a hat-trick of penalties in 1973?

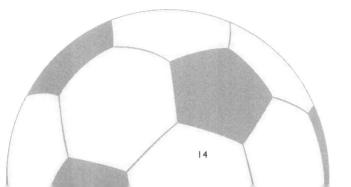

3   Which Hearts player famously stunned Ibrox by sitting
    on the ball during the build-up to a Hearts winning goal
    against Rangers?

4   Who was the first player to score more than 100 goals
    for Hearts?

5   Rudi Skacel scored in each of how many successive
    League matches from the start of the 2005–06 season?

6   Which player scored the goal that gave Hearts a positive
    points tally in season 2013–14, having started with a
    15-point deficit?

7   Which Hearts player scored a hat-trick in a 3–0 victory
    over Rangers at Ibrox in 1996 – the first visiting player
    at Ibrox to perform the feat since Alex Ferguson for
    St Johnstone thirty-three years earlier?

8   Which Hearts player had previously been a winner of the
    BBC's *Match of the Day* 'Goal of the Season' award?

9 In 1965, Hearts banged in 8 goals during an experimental match at Tynecastle on behalf of FIFA, in which offside was restricted. Who were the opponents and which player scored 5 goals that day?

10 Which player scored Hearts' 'Goal of the Season' for 2013–14 as awarded by the Hearts Youth Development Committee?

11 In an amazing 4–4 New Year draw with Hibs in 2003, Graham Weir scored twice in injury time as Hearts came back from 2 goals down. Who scored Hearts' other 2 goals that day?

Round 4

Hearts in Europe

'To see HMFC, we'll even dig the Channel Tunnel. Or go afloat on some big boat, and tie our scarves around the funnel.' So says the Hearts fans' European song. A bit outdated maybe, but still a huge favourite and sung with gusto around Europe – and we've had lots of fantastic Continental adventures along the way.

What do remember about our European encounters?

1 Who scored Hearts' first goal in European competition?

2 The mayor of which town came to Tynecastle for the second leg of a UEFA Cup match in 2003 in order to present the Hearts fans with an award for their exemplary behaviour during the away leg three weeks earlier?

3 Who scored Hearts' winning goal in that famous away victory?

4 Hearts played against which opponents in a European match in the Stade Olympique De La Pontaise?

5 In which stadium did Hearts initially refuse to play the away leg of a European Cup Winners Cup tie when, during the pre-match warm-up, they noticed that the crossbar at one end of the pitch was closer to the ground in the middle than at either end, and only agreed to kick off after lengthy negotiations with the UEFA delegate?

6   In 1976, Hearts stormed back from a 2–0 first-leg deficit
    to Lokomotiv Leipzig in the European Cup Winners'
    Cup by winning 5–1 in the return fixture. Which player –
    who made 217 competitive appearances for the club but
    scored only 3 goals – gave Hearts the lead that night
    with a 20-yard rocket and opened the floodgates?

7   Which Hearts striker was denied making his European
    debut in the San Siro stadium because his headmaster
    would not allow him to take time off school?

8   In what circumstances were Hearts eliminated from the
    1965–66 Inter-Cities Fairs Cup by the Spanish club
    Real Zaragoza?

9   In 2011, Hearts played against Paksi of Hungary in the
    Europa League. Due to the unsuitability of Paksi's own
    ground, the away leg was switched to the Sóstói Stadion,
    the home of which prominent Hungarian club?

10 Robbie Neilson memorably scored the 89th-minute winner in a 2–1 away Europa League victory over the Swiss club FC Basel in November 2004. But who scored Hearts' opening goal during the first half at St Jacob Park?

11 David Templeton scored the goal that gave Hearts their second-leg lead against Liverpool in a Europa League Play-Off tie at Anfield in August 2012. Who was the Liverpool goalkeeper who fumbled his shot?

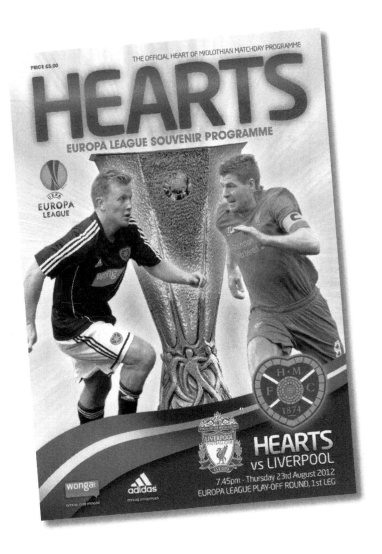

The Buck Stops Here

Who'd be a manager? They all tell you that when they are appointed, they set off in the sure knowledge that they are going to get the sack! They are the guys who have to take all the flak when things go wrong and take the bullet at the end of it. Then again, there is always the chance of leading out the team at Hampden and lifting a trophy, and that makes it all worthwhile. (Doesn't it?)

At Tynecastle, we've had managers who have become legends and some who have been unpopular from start to finish. What do you remember about these 'gaffers'?

1   Who succeeded the legendary Hearts manager, John McCartney, when he left his post in 1919?

2 Which Hearts manager once scored 3 goals in a European final?

3 And which Hearts manager missed the decisive penalty in a shoot-out in a European final?

4 Which Hearts manager was later appointed as manager of Apollon Limassol but was sacked after just 2 matches?

5 Which Hearts manager was the only Scottish player to have scored in the final stages of three World Cups?

6 What role had William McCartney filled in football before being appointed manager of Hearts?

7 Which manager has the dubious distinction of achieving the worst record in the club's history, consisting of no wins in 6 matches during a reign that lasted only twenty-eight days?

8 Which opposing manager accused Hearts boss John Robertson of kicking him after the final whistle of a UEFA Cup match in 2004?

9 Which player was appointed as temporary manager during the summer of 1995 and took charge for 3 pre-season matches – resulting in a 6–0 win, a 4–0 win and a 3–3 draw – before his brief reign came to an end when Jim Jefferies was appointed as the new permanent boss in time for the start of the League season?

10 Which manager was sacked in 1980, with Hearts sitting top of the table at the time?

11 Who is the only Hearts manager to win the prestigious Scottish Football Writers' Manager of the Year award?

Hearts Against the 'Wee Team'

'**C**an you hear the Hibees sing? No-oh, no-oh!' Is there a better sound than the roar of a goal celebration in the away end at Easter Road, accompanied by total silence in the rest of the stadium? I doubt it.

The derby match against Edinburgh's 'wee team' has to be the most passionate fixture on the Hearts calendar – and don't we just look forward to taking the next 3 points from them? OK, they've won a few, but we're streets in front – and what about those long, unbeaten runs!

This section is dead straightforward – just like beating our 'friends' from Leith.

1   How many derby matches did Hearts win in season 2013–14?

2   Who captained Hearts to a 3–1 victory against Hibs in the 1896 Scottish Cup final?

HIBERNIAN FOOTBALL CLUB

Bank of Scotland Premier League

HIBERNIAN V HEARTS
Sunday 15th October 2006 2pm

SOUTH STAND UPPER
ROW   SEAT
JJ   60
AWAY SUPPORT (SOUTH STAND)

X ENTER TURNSTILE 1-2   ADULT 25.00

3 Paul Hartley memorably scored a hat-trick against Hibs in the 4–0 Scottish Cup semi-final victory at Hampden Park in 2006. Who scored Hearts' other goal that day?

4 In January 2009, Hearts knocked Hibs out of the Scottish Cup with a 2–0 victory at Easter Road. Which two players scored their only Scottish Cup goals for Hearts that day?

5 What was the score in the first derby match between Hearts and Hibs?

6 Which player played a one-two with Neil Janczyck before slotting the ball into the Hibs net in the 90th minute to complete a late, late comeback from a goal down to win 2–1 at Easter Road in November 2002?

7   What nickname did Hibs fans give to the day in April 2014 when Hibs came to Tynecastle intending to be the team that relegated Hearts, only to suffer a 2–0 defeat themselves?

8   What was significant about Hearts' 2–1 victory over Hibs at Tynecastle on 1 April 1989?

9   On 21 May 2000, Hearts clinched their place in Europe by beating Hibs 2–1 at Tynecastle. Which player scored the winning goal?

10 After losing 3–2 to Hearts in a Boxing Day match, the Hibs manager infamously accused Hearts of being a 'pub team'. The words were pinned up in the Hearts dressing room as motivation before the next derby match and Hearts duly won 1–0 at Easter Road. Who was the offending Hibs manager?

11 How many goals did John Robertson ('The Hammer of the Hibs') score for Hearts against their Edinburgh rivals?

The Scottish Cup final between Hearts and Hibs on 19 May 2012 has deliberately been omitted from this section, as it was felt that the match deserved to have a chapter all of its own. Therefore, please see Round 22: The Greatest Game in History.

Round 7

For Club and Country

As the words of 'The Hearts Song' tell us:
'… and national caps we can always supply.'
From the earliest Scotland teams, Hearts have been no slouches when it comes to providing international players – and not only those being cheered on by the Tartan Army. We've had players capped by their countries the world over. Hearts managers down the years have spent sleepless nights worrying about players returning from international duty from all around the globe and whether they will come back fully fit for the club's next domestic fixture.

What do you remember about some of Tynecastle's international stars?

1 Which Hearts player postponed his honeymoon in May 2000 in order to answer a late call-up to the Scotland squad for a summer friendly match against the Republic of Ireland in Dublin, and ended up coming on as a substitute during added time?

2 Which three Hearts players made a combined total of
   19 appearances during Scotland's 9-match world tour of
   Israel, Hong Kong, Australia, New Zealand and Canada
   in 1967?

3 Who is the only player to have been capped by Wales
   while playing for Hearts?

4 Which member of Scotland's famous 'Wembley Wizards'
   team, which defeated England 5–1 at Wembley in 1928,
   was signed by Hearts two months later?

5 Who was the first Hearts player to be capped
   for Scotland?

6 Which player has scored most goals for Scotland while
   with Hearts?

7 Which non-Scottish player scored most goals for his
   country while he was a Hearts player? And which one
   won most caps?

8 Gary Mackay played 4 times for Scotland, scoring once. Which country did he score against and what was the major significance of his goal?

9 Who was the first Hearts goalkeeper to be capped for Scotland?

10 Which player signed for Hearts having previously won the European Championships while playing for his country?

11 Which three men have been appointed as manager of both Hearts and their own national teams?

Keep it in the Family

Supporting Hearts is often a case of having it in the blood – it's a family tradition. In some cases, the same can be said about playing the game professionally. Numerous Hearts players over the years have followed in their father's footsteps to become a professional player, produced a son who has done the same, or had a brother who also played the game. In some instances, both have even pulled on a maroon jersey.

In each of the following questions, find the Hearts player from the description of his well-known relative who was also a professional player.

1. His brother won 22 caps for Scotland and also won an English League and FA Cup double.

2. This player's son made 100 appearances for Celtic. Also played for Kilmarnock, Motherwell and Hibs.

3. His grandfather was a Hearts legend as a player and manager. Also scored a famous goal for Scotland against England at Wembley.

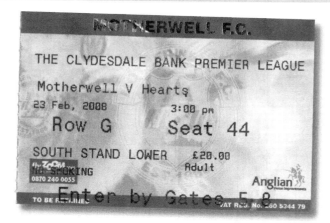

4 His brother was a striker who won the FA Cup and later became a presenter on the TV show *Gladiators*.

5 The father of this player managed several English clubs before coaching the Latvian national team and more recently, in his second spell with Yeovil Town, guided them to promotion to the English League Championship.

6 His brother played 8 times for Scotland, was the first Dundee United captain to lift a trophy and made 707 appearances for the Tannadice club.

7 This man's brother – a fellow defender – played alongside him for their first club, Dumbarton. They later faced each other as striker and defender in Old Firm matches for Celtic and Rangers.

8 His brother followed him into the first team at both Manchester City and Port Vale before going on to play for Birmingham City, Stoke City and Millwall.

9 His son also played for Hearts and represented Scotland at the 1992 European Championships.

10 The brother-in-law of this player made 130 competitive appearances for Hearts, having been bought from FC Metz, and scored 33 competitive goals, including 1 that secured a major trophy.

11 His son was a ball boy at Tynecastle before becoming a youth player at Hibs, but ultimately played a winning role in the all-Edinburgh Scottish Cup final of 2012.

Scottish Cup Glory

I t was first paraded in Edinburgh by horse and carriage and again more recently on an open-topped bus, with a throng of hundreds of thousands turning out along Princes Street and Gorgie Road to see the Scottish Cup being brought back home to Tynecastle.

We once had a drought of forty-three years without winning it, but now we've collected the oldest trophy still being played for in world football three times in the space of fourteen years.

Now wallow in Hearts' Scottish Cup glory.

1   The iconic image of the 1956 Scottish Cup final, in which Hearts defeated Celtic, is that of John Cumming ('The Iron Man') playing on with blood pouring from his bandaged head wound. With which Celtic player had he clashed heads?

2   How many goals did Hearts concede in their 1956 Scottish Cup-winning run?

3   Who did Hearts beat in the Scottish Cup final in 1906? And what colours did Hearts wear that day?

4 Who were the four penalty-takers in the shoot-out against Gretna as Hearts won the Scottish Cup final in 2006?

5 Who was the Hearts manager who guided his team to Scottish Cup glory in 2006?

6 Who was the captain of the first Hearts team to win the Scottish Cup – beating Dumbarton 1–0 in the 1891 final?

7 Who was Man of the Match in the 1998 Scottish Cup final, when Hearts defeated Rangers 2–1?

8 And who was the referee who awarded Hearts a first-minute penalty in this final?

9 When Hearts beat Hibs in the first all-Edinburgh Scottish Cup final in 1896, where was the match played, and whose home ground was it?

10 And what was the venue when Hearts beat Celtic 4–3 in the 1901 Scottish Cup Final?

11 Hearts required replays against both St Johnstone and St Mirren on their way to the 2012 Scottish Cup final. Which player scored in both replays?

For more on the 2012 Scottish Cup triumph, see Round 22: The Greatest Game in History.

The Legends

I t's a much overused word, though I'm sure there are a few players I've omitted from this section on Hearts legends whom some fans would have included. So please excuse me if I've missed out your particular favourite. But the guys here are the cream of the crop – the club's all-time heroes. In fact, each player mentioned in this section probably deserves a chapter all to himself.

(Note: Alfie Conn, Willie Bauld and Jimmy Wardhaugh are dealt with elsewhere in this book. Please see Round 19: The Terrible Trio.)

1 Which Hearts legend captained the side to a Scottish League Championship triumph, and later won three English FA Cups and was named Footballer of the Year in England?

2 Which club was Rudi Skacel playing for immediately before joining Hearts for his second spell at Tynecastle?

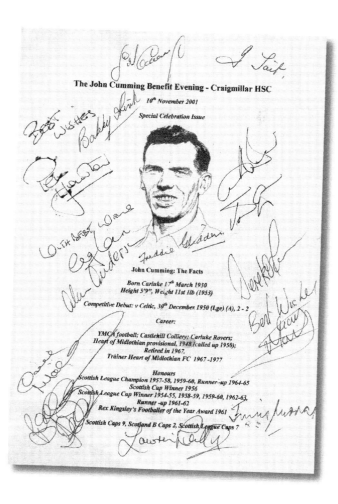

The John Cumming Benefit Evening - Craigmillar HSC

10th November 2001

Special Celebration Issue

John Cumming: The Facts

Born Carluke 17th March 1930
Height 5'9", Weight 11st 1lb (1953)

Competitive Debut: v Celtic, 30th December 1950 (Lge) (A), 2 - 2

Career:

YMCA football; Castlehill Colliery; Carluke Rovers;
Heart of Midlothian provisional, 1948 (called up 1950);
Retired in 1967.
Trainer Heart of Midlothian FC 1967 -1977

Honours
Scottish League Champion 1957-58, 1959-60, Runner-up 1964-65
Scottish Cup Winner 1956
Scottish League Cup Winner 1954-55, 1958-59, 1959-60, 1962-63,
Runner -up 1961-62
Rex Kingsley's Footballer of the Year Award 1961

Scottish Caps 9, Scotland B Caps 2, Scottish League Caps 7

3 Goalscoring legend Donald Ford won 3 caps for Scotland. Name two of the three countries he played against.

4 Barney Battles scored 218 goals in 200 competitive appearances for Hearts. He was capped only once for Scotland (he scored Scotland's goal in a 1–1 draw with Wales). But he was also capped by which other country?

5 Which Tynecastle legend won the highest number of major medals while playing for Hearts?

6 Which Hearts legend made 310 competitive appearances for the club and later became the manager of Hawick Royal Albert?

7 Where were Hearts playing a match at the time goalscoring legend John Robertson was being signed from Newcastle United?

8 Which monarch attended a Hearts match in 1912, especially because he wanted to watch Bobby Walker, who was reputed to be the best player in Europe at that time?

9   In the song 'Have You Seen The Heart Of Midlothian?'
    that first became popular on the terraces in the early
    1970s, which four legendary Hearts players are named
    as examples of the 'many famous heroes whose praises
    have been sung'?

10 Goalkeeper Jim Cruickshank (610 appearances;
    102 League clean sheets) famously made a triple save
    from a penalty kick against Hibs in 1967. Which Hibs
    player was denied three times?

11 Which Hearts legend was nicknamed 'The Blond
    Bombshell' at Tynecastle, going on to become a club
    legend in England, where he acquired a new nickname
    that was used as the title of a TV documentary
    about him?

Home is Where the Hearts Are

Tynecastle – our spiritual home. Hearts have resided here for more than 125 years. We've seen it packed to the rafters; we've revelled in spectacular European nights here under the floodlights. We've suffered ignominious failures too – but we wouldn't be without it. We've campaigned to save it from the bulldozers and we've rallied to prevent it from being sold off by the administrators.

But Tynecastle hasn't always been the home of the Hearts. From the club's earliest days, the team has played its home matches at a number of sites around Edinburgh. In this section, your knowledge about Hearts' various 'home grounds' is put under scrutiny.

1 Where did Hearts play their first home matches?

2 Tynecastle's main stand, erected in 1914, was designed by which famous sports architect? It was based on the main grandstand at an English club. Which one?

3 Where did Hearts play their home matches prior to moving to 'Old Tynecastle'?

4 Which was the first overseas club to play against Hearts at Tynecastle?

5 Which English club was defeated 2–1 in Hearts' final match at 'Old Tynecastle' in April 1886 before they moved across the road to the current site?

6 And which other English club travelled to Edinburgh to play against Hearts in the first match at the 'New Tynecastle' a few weeks later?

7 In 2004, Hearts made the controversial decision to play their home European matches at Murrayfield, the home of Scotland's national rugby union team. Who were the first opponents at that stadium and what was the score?

8 Which iconic feature of Tynecastle was added to the stadium in 1954 and remains (in a modified form) to this day?

9 Which world football legend described Tynecastle as 'a very special place to play football' when he said it was one of the most atmospheric grounds in Europe, having just seen Hearts defeat his team in a UEFA Cup match?

10 How many times has Tynecastle staged a full Scotland international match?

11 In 2000, Tynecastle was the venue for a Rugby League World Cup match involving which two countries?

Hearts Against the Auld Enemy

The best that England has to offer have ventured to Tynecastle and, although we have taken the odd beating, more often than not Hearts have 'sent them homeward tae think again'.

Border raids? No problem. We can win on Sassenach territory too.

We've taken on the Auld Enemy in European competition, friendly matches and pre-season tournaments. We've come face to face with them on overseas trips and come out on top. We've even played against them for the title of 'world champions'.

In this section, simply test your knowledge about memorable games against English opposition.

1   Following the 1958 League Championship-winning success, Hearts embarked on a tour of the USA and Canada. Which English team did they play against 4 times, recording 2 wins, 1 draw and 1 defeat?

2 Who did Hearts beat 4–0 at Wrigley Field, Los Angeles in 1960?

3 Having just won the Scottish Cup in 1998, Hearts played against Charlton Athletic at The Valley. Whose testimonial match was it?

4 After playing in their respective Scottish and English cup finals in 1976, Hearts played against FA Cup winners Southampton at The Dell a week later. Which Hearts player scored twice in a 3–2 victory?

5 What was the result when respective 1901 (Scottish and English) FA Cup winners Hearts and Tottenham Hotspur played against each other for the unofficial 'World Championship'?

6 Why did Hearts play a match against Stoke City at Tynecastle in 1964?

7 Who did Hearts play against in their only appearance in the English FA Cup, and what was the result?

8 In August 1990, Hearts participated in the pre-season 'Bucharest Tournament'. Which English team did they play against in the play-off match for 3rd and 4th place?

9 Hearts reached the final of the Texaco Cup in 1971, but lost 3–2 on aggregate to Wolverhampton Wanderers. However, they at least won the away leg 1–0 at Molineux. Who scored the winning goal for Hearts that night?

10　En route to that 1971 final, another English club was on the wrong end of a stirring Hearts comeback. After losing 3–1 away from home in the first leg, which team was defeated 4–1 at Tynecastle?

11　Hearts came from 2 goals down to defeat Fulham 3–2 in a pre-season match at Tynecastle in July 1999. Which latin favourite scored a spectacular winner for Hearts as he stole the limelight from a big-name striker who was making his debut for the London club? And who was the Fulham debutant?

Aye Aye, Cap'n

Captain Marvel or Captain Sensible? It takes all types to make a successful skipper – the all-action marauder who leads by example; the solid, dependable veteran who has seen it all; the fist-in-your-face motivator; the thoughtful, tactically astute organiser.

This round is simply all about the leaders of our gang.

1 Who did Tom Purdie defeat 3–2 in a one-a-side football match to decide who would become Hearts' first captain?

2 Which Hearts captain won 22 Scottish caps and ended his playing career with Swindon Town?

3 Which Hearts captain later became manager of the Australia national team?

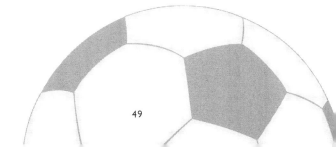

4   Freddie Glidden captained Hearts to victory in the 1956
    Scottish Cup final, but who was the regular captain that
    season and missed the final through injury?

5   Which former Hearts captain returned to the club
    in November 2013 as Youth Development Manager,
    and has since been promoted?

6   Which Hearts legend, who won 18 Scotland caps
    (11 with Hearts), was transferred to Aston Villa where
    he also became an iconic figure, subsequently their
    manager, and was known there as 'The Ace of Hearts'?

7   Which future Hearts captain arrived at Tynecastle in
    1996 in a £400,000 part-exchange deal, with John Millar
    moving in the opposite direction?

8 Which club captain has been the only player since the Second World War to have played for Hearts, then Hibs, then returned to Tynecastle – with no other club in between?

9 Which captain won 10 Scotland Under-21 caps between 1996 and 1997?

10 What distinction did the two captains have in common when Hearts played against Dunfermline in the 1968 Scottish Cup final?

11 Who became the youngest captain in the Scottish Premier League when he was appointed Hearts skipper in August 2007?

Just Champion

It hasn't happened for more than half a century, but at least Hearts can claim to have won the Scottish League Championship on four occasions. Older fans will still recall those triumphant days when the boys in maroon really were 'the best in the land'. You may not have been around at the time, but if you know your history, you'll know all about our title-winning years.

1   Hearts won the League in season 1957–58 with a record tally of 132 goals, a figure which no other team has come close to emulating. Who scored goal number 132?

2   Hearts scored in 33 of their 34 League matches that season. Which was the only club to prevent them from finding the net?

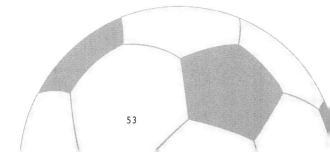

3 Against which club was the title clinched that year, and with how many games to spare?

4 Name the only club to defeat Hearts on their way to winning the League Championship in 1957–58.

5 What was the winning points margin in the 1957–58 Championship triumph?

6 Which player was top scorer as Hearts won the title again in 1959–60?

7 Against whom did Hearts clinch the title this time?

8 Hearts' first League title was claimed in 1894–95, the club having kicked off the season by winning how many matches in succession?

9 Which was the only club to defeat Hearts in the League that season?

10 At the start of the 1959–60 Championship-winning
     season, manager Tommy Walker signed a well-known
     player and 12,000 fans turned up to watch him play in
     his first reserve match. Which player?

11 Hearts won their second title in 1897 by beating Clyde
     5–0 in their final League match of the season, having
     started the day level on points with which club?

Round

15

Get a Move On

Who came from where? And which club did we sell him to? They're the usual memory tests we put to each other on those away trips. But not all transfers are as straightforward as they seem.

Can you remember the finer details about some of Hearts' transfer activity (or non-activity) and the comings and goings of these players who have passed through Tynecastle?

1 Which player bought out his contract with his previous club in order to sign for Hearts in 2007 and which club did he come from?

2 Which player changed his nationality in order to sign for Hearts in 2009?

3   A transfer embargo was imposed on Hearts in June 1982 due to unpaid transfer fees for which two players?

4   Who was the first player to leave Tynecastle on a Bosman-style transfer and which club did he join?

5   In 1968, Hearts sold a defender to the English League Champions for a fee that was a record for both clubs at the time. Who was the player and which club did he join?

6   Ryan McGowan left Hearts to join which Chinese club during the 2012–13 season?

7   In 2006, a Hearts player became the first footballer to invoke a FIFA transfer regulation that allowed a player to cancel his contract in the third year of a four-year contract, providing he joined a club in another country. Who was the player and which club did he join?

8   Which Hearts player travelled to Dundee United on transfer deadline day in 2005 to undertake a medical, only to be called back at the last minute by Hearts because the board had changed their minds about sanctioning the transfer?

9 Why did twenty-five members of the Hearts playing staff, including the first team, hand in transfer requests in October 1979?

10 When Tynecastle legend Alex Young was transferred to Everton in 1960, which Hearts teammate also moved to Goodison Park at the same time for a fee of £180,000?

11 When Hearts bought Dave McPherson from Rangers in 1987, which Ibrox teammate came with him as part of the same deal?

Round 16

Jambograms

OK, we've had some serious stuff. Now it's puzzle time – well, football is supposed to be fun, isn't it? So here's a chance to get your cryptic brain cells working. This section should be a doddle for all you crossword lovers. Just solve the anagrams of these famous Hearts players' names – with an additional clue to help you.

All the answers are the names of players who have won at least one major medal while playing for Hearts.

1 **MA'S GOLF HOTEL**

Did he waltz his way to a medal?

2 **SMOOTH GRIND**

But never a grinder – and definitely not third choice!

3 **WIDE IF FULL**

Very few got past him.

4 **KISSY IS FAST**

Especially on the overlap.

5 **ANGRY IN GARDEN**

He was no shrinking violet when put on the spot.

6 **NO MORE HOT EGGS**

He was poached down south.

7 **A DIVA BRIDE**

Perfect on pitch, he reached the high notes with Hearts, and had no problem hitting a treble.

8 **ORDER AND VISION**

The keys to a Hampden victory perhaps?

9 **I'M A BRILL HAT**

A topper, presumably.

10 **COW MA GRANNY**

… but don't be a bull in a china shop.

11 **SOULLESS TIGER**

Roared back after a Hampden nightmare.

Round

17

As Low as it Gets

We've paid tribute to the greats, revelled in our successes and wallowed in nostalgia. But this wouldn't be a true quiz book about Hearts if we didn't include the painful episodes – and let's face it, if you've never had your heart broken, you've never been a Hearts fan.

We've suffered relegation (even though it took 103 years in coming), we've almost gone out of existence and we've sat on the terracing and shed tears after having major triumphs snatched from our grasp.

So here's another batch of questions to get out of the way quickly before we celebrate the good times again.

1   In April 1977, Hearts were relegated from the top flight for the first time in a history that, at that point, had stretched back 103 years. What was the result of the match that confirmed the drop into the old Second Division?

2   Relegation followed again in 1979, after just 1 season back in the top flight. In a calamitous run, Hearts finished their League campaign with how many successive defeats and by how many points did they finish below survival?

3   In April 1965, Hearts went into the final day of the League season on top of the table, needing only to avoid a 2–0 defeat by Kilmarnock at home in order to be confirmed as Scottish Champions. The visitors duly won 2–0 to claim the title. What was the margin that finally separated the two teams at the top of the table?

4   Relegation from the SPFL Premiership was confirmed in April 2014, despite Hearts winning away from home on the same day – against which opponents?

5 The 7–0 home defeat by Hibs on New Year's Day 1973 was a result which still haunts many Hearts fans. Both teams had been challenging for leadership of the First Division table going into the festive period, and Hearts had conceded only 3 goals in their previous 9 home matches since the start of that season. Which former Hearts favourite rubbed salt into the wound by scoring twice that day?

6 Relegation was suffered for a third time in the club's history at the end of the 1980–81 campaign – probably Hearts' worst ever League performance, as they finished bottom of the Premier League table. How many victories had been achieved in their 36 League matches?

7 Probably the most disappointing result for many current Hearts fans was the 2–0 defeat by Dundee at Dens Park on the final day of the 1985–86 season, which cost the Tynecastle club the League title. The team had been struck by a virus in the days leading up to the match and defender Craig Levein, suffering from a gastro-intestinal bug, did not recover in time. Which player came in to replace him – the only change to a winning side – and, despite the result, was highly praised for his sterling performance?

8 In 2004, Hearts were in grave danger of losing their much-loved Tynecastle. Chief executive Chris Robinson required police protection from angry Hearts fans following a stormy AGM in September, in which shareholders voted in favour of selling the stadium (in spite of 73 per cent refusing to vote). Which house-building company entered an agreement to buy the stadium and what was the agreed price?

9   When Hearts entered administration in June 2013,
    they were ordered to begin the following season with a
    deficit of how many points?

10 Well, Hearts won one never-to-be forgotten Scottish Cup
    final 5–1 – but also lost one by the same score. Which
    opponent scored a hat-trick that day in 1996?

11 When Hearts were faced with a winding-up order over
    an unpaid tax bill in November 2012, the club warned
    that their next match could be their last, as Heart of
    Midlothian FC was in danger of going out of business.
    Who were the opponents in that game and what was
    the score?

Round

18

Under
Starter's Orders

Well, we all have to start somewhere, don't we?
So this section is all about players making their
debuts for Hearts, with varying degrees of
success. Some have made an instant impact; others have
probably wished they could go back and start again. But, then,
it's not how you start; it's how you finish – isn't it?

1 All-time leading scorer John Robertson made his Hearts
debut alongside his brother Chris in 1982 – their only
appearance together. Who were the opponents?

2 Which player, signed on loan in 1999, played the first
45 minutes of an SPL match against Dundee at Dens Park,
was replaced at half-time, and was never seen again?

3 Who scored within 50 seconds of his debut in a 2–1 win at
Aberdeen in 1978?

HEART OF MIDLOTHIAN

PRICE
6D

OFFICIAL PROGRAMME

EINTRACHT EDITION

Hearts heisst SG Eintracht Frankfurt
herzlichst in Edinburgh willkommen

Goalkeeper HANS TILKOWSKI in action

CHALLENGE MATCH

HEART OF MIDLOTHIAN
v
EINTRACHT FRANKFURT
AT TYNECASTLE PARK
Monday, 14th April, 1969
KICK-OFF 7.30 P.M.

4 Donald Ford scored 4 times in a 5–0 Texaco Cup victory over Airdrie at Broomfield in 1970, but which teammate also scored on his Hearts debut that night?

5 After having four defenders sent off against Rangers at Ibrox in 1996, emergency measures were required to form a rearguard for a League Cup quarter-final against Celtic the following midweek. Which English Premier League player was signed on a non-contract basis and played only in that game?

6 And which future internationalist made his debut in that 1–0 victory over Celtic?

7 Which legendary Hearts goalkeeper later recalled his debut – a 2–0 defeat by Falkirk at Brockville – and said, 'I stood there in the mud and the rain, and thought to myself, "What the f*** am I doing here?"'

8 In August 2002, Mark de Vries marked his full debut by scoring 4 goals in a 5–1 defeat of Hibs at Tynecastle to become an instant Tynecastle hero. Which club had Hearts signed him from?

9 Michael Ngoo, signed on loan from Liverpool, made his Hearts debut in 2013 and scored in the Scottish League Cup semi-final against Inverness Caledonian Thistle. He also found the net during the penalty shoot-out that took the team to the final. What shirt number was he wearing?

10 Which Hearts favourite of the 1970s marked his debut by scoring 2 goals in a 4–1 win over Dunfermline at East End Park in September 1971?

11 In the 1996–97 European Cup Winners Cup, Hearts were drawn to play against Red Star Belgrade, who had been European champions just five years earlier. Which newly signed internationalist made his competitive debut in the away leg, when Hearts battled to a creditable goalless draw, only to eventually be eliminated on the away goals rule?

The Terrible Trio

Alfie Conn, Willie Bauld, Jimmy Wardhaugh. An inside forward trio that formed the most devastating goalscoring act in Scottish football and the very mention of their names brings glorious memories flooding back to those who were fortunate enough to see them play. Although I was born just too late to remember watching them in action, I was brought up listening to tales of 'The Terrible Trio', courtesy of a Hearts-mad father.

From the moment they were teamed up together in a Hearts side that had been struggling, until Bauld's final appearance in 1962, they brought terror to opposing defences and played a huge part in bringing trophies to Tynecastle.

Their individual records are remarkable (Conn – played 407, goals 219; Bauld – played 510, goals 356; Wardhaugh – played 517, goals 375). Together, they were unstoppable.

What do you know about the Trio?

1   All three members of the Terrible Trio played for
    Scotland, but which one was not actually born
    in Scotland?

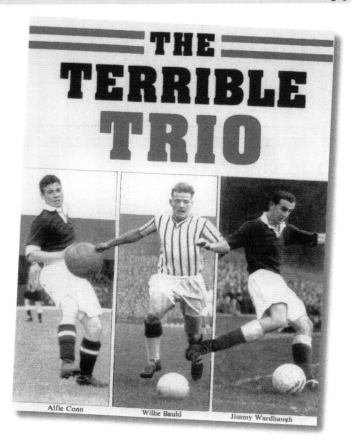

THE
TERRIBLE
TRIO

Alfie Conn   Willie Bauld   Jimmy Wardhaugh

2   Against which opponents did Alfie Conn make his only
    appearance for Scotland?

3   Which major English club cancelled Willie Bauld's
    registration before he arrived at Tynecastle?

4 Which manager was the first to play all three of them together in the Hearts first team, thereby launching the Terrible Trio?

5 Who were the opponents that day and what was the score?

6 Wardhaugh did his National Service with which branch of the armed services?

7 Which non-footballing occupation did Bauld and Conn share before blooming into top-class footballers?

8 What was Jimmy Wardhaugh's nickname among Hearts supporters?

9 Which modern-day footballer was Sir Alex Ferguson talking about in 2013 when he said he had never seen such a great header of the ball since Willie Bauld?

10 Alfie Conn had a brief spell as player-manager of which club in South Africa?

11 Which member of the Trio became a sports journalist after his career in football ended?

They Shall Not Grow Old

I t was the saddest and most emotional period in Hearts' history. It was also the proudest. And no book about the Tynecastle club would be complete without paying tribute to the team that perished during the First World War.

At a time when the national press and certain Members of Parliament were railing against the continuation of professional football throughout Britain during the conflict with Germany and the reluctance of clubs to release their fit, young footballers from their contracts in order to join the army, the Hearts first team led by example, volunteering en masse for active service during the early months of the war. They were the only football team in Britain to do so, and took more than 600 shareholders and season ticket holders with them, thus raising an entire battalion in a record time of six days.

Ironically, manager John McCartney had just finished building the team which was probably the best ever to wear the maroon jerseys and, at the time, was reputed to be the best in Britain.

They had romped to the top of the Scottish League, with most of Scotland willing them to take the title ahead of the Old Firm. But with the prize tantalisingly in sight, the rigours of army training and unavailability of players took their toll; they fell agonisingly short and lost the title to a full-strength Celtic side which had not given up a single player to the armed forces.

On the battlefields of France and Belgium, some also lost their lives. Others were severely wounded and never played football again. It took Hearts almost forty years to recover from the loss of this great team and their comrades.

A crowd of 40,000 were in attendance as the Hearts war memorial was unveiled at Haymarket in 1922 for the club's first Remembrance Service, an event which has been held annually to this day.

'These fine young men', as McCartney described them, must never be forgotten. This section is dedicated to those Hearts players and fans who made the supreme sacrifice.

1 How many successive League matches did Hearts win from the start of the 1914–15 season?

2 How many Hearts players were in army uniform by Christmas of that season?

3 Which Edinburgh venue staged a recruiting rally as hundreds of the club's supporters joined the players to enlist en masse?

4 Which army unit did most of the players join?

5 As army training took its toll, along with unavailability of players, results suffered during the second half of the season and the march towards an almost certain League Championship was halted as only 1 point was gained from the final 3 fixtures. Having topped the table for thirty-five out of thirty-seven weeks, how many points did Hearts eventually finish behind Celtic?

6 What is the name of the village in France which the Hearts players helped to briefly capture from the enemy on the first day of the Battle of the Somme, and where a cairn now stands as a memorial?

7 Hearts manager John McCartney was in regular touch with 'his sons' from Tynecastle while they were on active service. What other full-time job did he take on to supplement his income while on a reduced Hearts salary during the conflict?

8 What was the title of the booklet that John McCartney wrote about the players who volunteered?

9 How many Hearts players died during active service?

10 Which player suffered during a gas attack in the trenches, never fully recovered and died after collapsing with a heart attack while appearing as a guest player for Hearts during an exhibition match in 1926?

11 Which dignitary unveiled the Hearts war memorial at Haymarket on the occasion of the club's first annual Remembrance Service, attended by 40,000 people in 1922?

They Shall Not Pass

There are thirty rounds in this quiz book, and not a single one about goalkeepers' clangers. Why? Because Hearts fans have been really spoiled over many years. We've had some of the best goalkeepers in the business between our sticks. Many have gone on to become Tynecastle legends. OK, we've seen the occasional dipstick, but fortunately they have not lasted long – so let's focus on the good ones rather than struggle to remember eleven howlers. What do you know about the men who have served as Hearts' last line of defence?

1 Jamie MacDonald saved a penalty by which Tottenham Hotspur player during a Europa League play-off match at White Hart Lane in 2011?

2 Kenny Garland left Hearts in 1975 after nine years with the club to pursue which career outside football?

3 Who was the first goalkeeper to play in 100 matches for Hearts?

4   Craig Gordon became a £9 million player when he was sold to Sunderland in 2007, a British record fee for a goalkeeper at the time. Which club had he played for on loan as a teenager before establishing himself in the Hearts first team?

5   Full-back Lee Wallace became an emergency goalkeeper in a match against Inverness Caledonian Thistle after which Hearts goalkeeper had been sent off, all three substitutes having already been used?

6   Which goalkeeper has kept a record number of clean sheets for Hearts, and who was the manager who signed him?

7   In November 2010, at a home match against Hamilton Academical, Hearts paid tribute to legendary goalkeeper Jim Cruickshank, who had died that week. Which keeper of the day tied a replica of Cruickshank's favourite yellow jersey to the back of his net that afternoon and proceeded to save a penalty which preserved his clean sheet, later saying that he was sure that Cruickie had been looking down on him?

8   Which Hearts goalkeeper saved 2 penalties in a match against Hibs at Easter Road in 1974? He also saved 3 in a reserve game against the same opposition.

9 What nationality was Anthony Basso, who played in
   8 competitive matches for Hearts in 2007–08?

10 Which goalkeeper kept 13 clean sheets in 31 League
   appearances during Hearts' Championship-winning run
   of 1957–58?

11 Name two Hearts goalkeepers who have also played in
   post-war English FA Cup finals.

Round

22

The Greatest Game in History

According to one of the popular Hearts songs, it's 'the game on New Year's Day'. That all changed on Saturday, 19 May 2012.

The first all-Edinburgh Scottish Cup final since 1896, the first to be played at Hampden and only the second in history. It was the derby clash to end all derbies. The one that would provide bragging rights for all time. The one that would cancel out all other derby boasts. And we all know how it ended – Hearts 5, Hibs 1. (You didn't really think that was going to be one of the questions, did you?)

We've already had a section on Edinburgh derbies, but we couldn't publish a Hearts quiz book without including a complete section on the most important derby of them all – well, could we?

1 Name the Hearts starting line-up.

2 How many minutes did it take for Hearts to score their first goal?

3 Who was the referee in the final?

4 Which two players in the Hearts line-up had captained their teams in previous Scottish Cup finals?

5 Name the scorers of Hearts' 5 goals.

6 Which four Hearts players were playing their last game for the club?

7 Which Hearts player was tripped, leading to the award of a penalty in the second half?

8 Why was Hibs manager Pat Fenlon sent to the stand by the referee?

9 Which player was named as the sponsors' Man of the Match?

10 Which three Hearts substitutes made their appearance in the second half?

11 The cup final was to be Hearts manager Paulo Sergio's last match in charge of the team. He left Tynecastle to manage which club?

The World at Our Feet

How many different nationalities have been represented at Hearts? Too tough a question? OK, I'll tell you. At the time of writing there have been forty-six, if you count all the home nations separately. Like most clubs in the UK nowadays, Tynecastle has resembled something of a mini United Nations, with the conveyor belt of Lithuanians that has passed through Gorgie during the Romanov era merely adding to the international flavour of the club.

We've had players from all over the world – but what do you remember of the following?

1   Who was the first Lithuanian player to play for Hearts?

2   Who was the first overseas player to turn out for Hearts since the Second World War?

3   Which overseas player has played most matches for Hearts?

4   And which one has scored most goals?

5 Hearts have had several South American players in their ranks, but only one player each from Brazil, Argentina and Chile. Can you name the player in question in each case?

6 Which player arrived at Tynecastle with a Champions League winner's medal?

7 Cult favourite Pasquale Bruno was signed from which club in 1995?

8 David Obua, who arrived at Tynecastle in 2008 and stayed with Hearts for almost four years, had won a League title and been voted Player of the Year in which country?

9 Which Tynecastle cult favourite of the 1990s left his home country as a 10 year old after Benfica offered him a scholarship at their football academy and never returned for nineteen years because of civil conflict in his homeland?

10 Which midfield player was signed on a free transfer from the French club, Sedan, in September 2002 and played in only 3 matches (he was substituted in 2 of them) before being freed the following summer?

11 Which player, who grew up in Edinburgh but was born in South Africa, played for Hearts during the 1980s and 1990s, and later became a TV presenter on the men's lifestyle satellite channel Men & Motors?

A Hiding to Nothing

They are the cup draws that everyone wants, but dreads at the same time – being paired against a lower division side which should be a pushover and lead to an easy route into the next round. If you win, it's only what you were expected to do. Lose and you suffer the ignominy of being the victim of a giant-killing act.

Like every other senior club, Hearts have had their fair share of coming a cropper against minnows. In this section, we recall some of those cup ties that have pitted Hearts against potential giant-killers. Some have been dispatched as a matter of routine, others have provided us with some scary moments en route to scraping through. Then there are those which have resulted in complete embarrassment! What do you remember about the following David v. Goliath affairs?

I   The late John Fairgrieve, celebrated newspaper journalist and well-known Hearts fan, once wrote that Tynecastle should be turned into a car park after his beloved team had been knocked out of the Scottish Cup by which lower-division team in 1982?

2 Hearts scraped through against non-league Auchinleck Talbot on their way to winning the Scottish Cup in 2012. Who scored the decisive goal in a 1–0 victory at Tynecastle?

3 Which player scored a hat-trick as Hearts defeated Alloa Athletic 4–0 in a Scottish League Cup match at Recreation Park in September 2006?

4 Hearts were heading out of the Scottish Cup as they trailed Montrose 1–0 at Links Park in 1970. Which player scored an injury-time equaliser to perform a rescue act, then also scored the only goal of the replay – also in the dying moments?

5 Hearts were paired with Montrose again in the Scottish Cup in 1976. This time it took 3 matches before they edged past the Second Division side. After drawing 2–2 for the second time, the decider was won 2–1 after extra time. Which neutral venue was used for the third match?

6 Hearts were knocked out of the Scottish League Cup by Ayr United in a penalty shoot-out at Somerset Park in September 2011. Which two Hearts players missed from the penalty spot?

7 Which Second Division team did Hearts beat 4–1 on their way to the Scottish Cup final in 1968?

8 Inverness Caledonian Thistle have been a major force
   in the Scottish Premier League in recent seasons.
   But when Hearts played against them in a Scottish
   Cup tie at Tynecastle in January 1985, they were still
   a Highland League team. Which Hearts player scored
   4 goals in that match and what was the final score?

9 Which other Highland League club were beaten in the
   Scottish Cup in 1993 and what was the score?

10 In October 1999, Hearts defeated East Fife 2–0 in a
   Scottish League Cup tie. As East Fife's ground was being
   rebuilt, where was the match played and which new
   French signing made his Hearts debut that night?

11 Which Hearts player scored a hat-trick in a 4–0
   Scottish Cup win at Stranraer in January 2007?

The Scottish League Cup

Maybe it's only Scotland's 'wee cup' – but the Scottish League Cup has a special place in Hearts' history. For a start, the first time we won it, the victory ended a barren spell of forty-eight years without a major trophy coming to Tynecastle.

This section is all about the triumphs, the near misses and the failures in Hearts' League Cup adventures.

1 Who is Hearts' record goalscorer in League Cup matches?

2 Who was the only non-British player to score for Hearts on the run that took the club to the Scottish League Cup final in 2012–13?

3 How did Hearts become the architects of their own downfall in the 1969–70 Scottish League Cup competition?

4   Who did Hearts defeat in the final when they won the Scottish League Cup for the first time?

5   Which player scored on his Hearts debut against Stenhousemuir on the way to the 1996 Scottish League Cup final?

6   Which Hearts player scored a hat-trick in the 1954 Scottish League Cup final?

7   And who scored the winning goal in the 1959 Scottish League Cup final?

8   Which venue hosted the 1996 Scottish League Cup final between Hearts and Rangers, and what was the reason for this choice?

9   In the 2013 Scottish League Cup final, which player lined up to play against his former club?

10   Which club defeated Hearts in a penalty shoot-out after a 4–4 draw in the League Cup quarter-final of 1995?

11   Which player scored both Hearts goals in a memorable 2–0 League Cup victory over Celtic at Parkhead in 2007?

Loan Stars

Neither a borrower nor a lender be, they say. It has sometimes been short and sweet, but Hearts have borrowed plenty of players over the years. We've lent out a few gems, too.

These questions are all about the players we've had on loan from other clubs, and some who have been farmed out for a while.

1 When Ricardo Fuller joined Hearts on loan in 2001, what was his parent club?

2 Who was the first player brought to Tynecastle on loan during the January transfer window after the club's transfer embargo was lifted during the 2012–13 season?

3 Which player, who had been on loan at Hearts, later left his job in London as a TV director and cameraman, filming naked women for the TV channel Babestation (he described it as 'the best job in the world') in order to return to Scotland and play junior football for Bellshill?

4 Who was the first player to sign for Hearts on loan?

5 Goalkeeper Jamie MacDonald enjoyed a successful
loan period with which club before returning to
Tynecastle and establishing himself as the regular
first-team keeper?

6 Which defender came to Hearts on loan from
Bradford City and now has a cocktail named after him
(it's a mixture of Orange Aftershock and Red Bull, and is
a speciality in Tappie Toories bar in Dunfermline)?

7 Having become a Hearts legend by scoring the goal
which knocked Hibs out of the Scottish Cup in 1994,
Wayne Foster ended his Tynecastle career by playing
4 matches on loan at which English club?

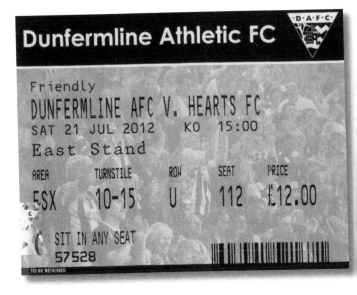

8   Which young Hearts player spent loan spells with
    Cowdenbeath and Queen of the South before returning
    to Tynecastle, winning the Scottish Cup and eventually
    becoming club captain?

9   Which English Premier League striker spent the second
    half of the 2013–14 season on loan at Hearts, but
    started only 4 matches and failed to score?

10 Which goalkeeper, who initially joined Hearts on
    loan in 2003, but later signed permanently, was a
    Finnish international?

11 Which player was loaned to Alloa Athletic and helped
    them win promotion in 2011–12 before joining the
    Hearts first-team squad the following season?

Never Go Back

t's a phrase that can never be true about going back to Tynecastle, of course! Of all the players who have returned to Hearts after sampling life elsewhere, none could ever be accused of being a glutton for punishment, could they? It's more a case of 'absence makes the heart grow fonder'.

Use the following eleven clues to identify eleven players who have played for Hearts, left Tynecastle, and returned at a later date for a second spell with the club.

1   Began playing career at Gartcosh United, finished it with Morton, where he was also the manager. In between, won 27 caps for Scotland and played in all 3 group matches at the 1990 World Cup finals and 1992 European Championship finals. Scottish Cup winner with Hearts.

2   Highlander who also played shinty as a youth, but joined Hearts as a winger. Manager Alex MacDonald brought him back for his second spell. Later became a highly respected coach and SFA's Head of Coaching.

3 Scored in two Scottish Cup finals. Hearts' top scorer in three separate seasons. Initially signed from Marseille.

4 Champions League campaigner who volunteered to take a substantial cut in salary so that he could go on loan to his boyhood favourites.

5 Emerged from Chelsea's Youth Academy before returning to Scotland to begin his senior career. Scored twice in a cup final.

6 Played once for Scotland – against Finland. Jock Stein once described him as having talent comparable to Kenny Dalglish. Among other clubs, he also played for Sheffield United, Aston Villa and Middlesbrough.

7 Won 26 caps for Scotland. Was named as Man of the Match in a cup final, despite ending up on the losing side. After leaving Tynecastle for the second time, he scored against Hearts on his debut for his new club.

8 Won 2 caps for Scotland – against Malta and Saudi Arabia – and was subsequently elected as Rector of the University of Edinburgh.

9   Made his Hearts debut while still a schoolboy at George Heriot's School. The only player to have played for both Edinburgh and both Dundee clubs.

10 In between his two spells for Hearts, he played in the 1987 UEFA Cup final, 4 Scottish Cup finals, 4 Scottish League Cup finals and won one Scottish League title.

11 Played 16 times for Scotland. Commanded a record transfer fee of £725,000 when he left Hearts the first time. Went on loan to Dundee before finishing his playing career as player-coach at Livingston.

The Record Breakers

The biggest, the youngest, the best, the most prolific. This is a straightforward round, all about Hearts' record-breakers. Who scored the most, who cost the most, etc. Get your thinking caps on.

1 Which player holds the record for captaining the Hearts team in the highest number of matches?

2 Which player holds the record for making the most international appearances for Scotland while at Hearts?

3 What is the record fee that Hearts have paid for a player, who was he and which club did they sign him from?

4 Which player has scored most goals in a season for Hearts and what was his total?

5 John Robertson is Hearts' all-time record League goalscorer with a total of 271. Against whom did he score his last goal for Hearts?

6 Who is the youngest player to have played in a competitive match for Hearts, becoming the youngest player in SPL history in the process, and what age was he?

7 What is the record victory in a derby match between Hearts and Hibs?

8 Which Hearts record-breaker was known at Tynecastle as 'The Janitor'?

9 Which player holds the dubious distinction of having been sent off on most occasions while playing for Hearts?

10 The highest attendance for a Hearts match at Tynecastle was recorded in which season?

11 A crowd of 98,208 was the largest for a Hearts match that did not involve either Rangers or Celtic. Who were the opponents and what was the occasion?

Round 29

Bad Boys

I t wouldn't be football if there wasn't a controversy for us to argue about afterwards, would it? So we need a villain. We've come across plenty of those – and supplied a few of our own as well. From fisticuffs in the tunnel to dodgy referees and linesmen, from scoundrels in suits to rebellious players who have fallen foul of the manager. We've seen them all.

Can you remember this rogues' gallery?

1 Saulius Mikoliunus was sent off for pushing over a linesman during a home match against Rangers in March 2005 after he had signalled for an outrageous penalty. Who was the infamous linesman that night?

2 Manager Craig Levein was handed a four-month touchline ban after his continued refusal to pay a twice-doubled fine following his criticism of the performance of which referee in a match against Kilmarnock in 2003?

3 Jamie Hamill was suspended for pushing which opposing manager to the ground during a goal celebration in April 2014?

4 Which player, who had won 8 caps for France and was French Player of the Year in season 1987–88, joined Hearts later in his career but was released by the club in 1997 after failing a drugs test?

5 Which four Hearts players were all sent off during the second half of a match against Rangers at Ibrox in September 1996?

6 Julian Brellier was sent off for a second bookable offence in a Champions League qualifier against AEK Athens in August 2006. For what unusual offence did he receive his first yellow card?

7 What punishment did manager Craig Levein mete out to Graham Weir and Neil Janczyk after they broke team orders by playing golf twenty-four hours before an Edinburgh derby in 2004?

8 As Hearts lost 2–1 to Hamilton Academicals in a Scottish Premier League match at New Douglas Park in December 2009, four Hearts players, team masseur Alan Robson and Hamilton player Leon Knight were all shown red cards – either on the field or during a post-match brawl in the tunnel. Who were the four Hearts players involved?

9 Why was team captain Walter Kidd sent off during the 1986 Scottish Cup final against Aberdeen?

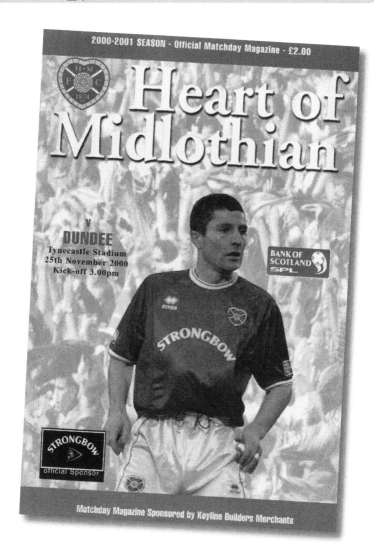

2000-2001 SEASON - Official Matchday Magazine - £2.00

Heart of Midlothian

V
DUNDEE
Tynecastle Stadium
25th November 2000
Kick-off 3.00pm

BANK OF SCOTLAND
SPL

STRONGBOW

STRONGBOW
official Sponsor

Matchday Magazine Sponsored by Keyline Builders Merchants

10 Which two Hearts players clashed with each other in a
    punch-up at a 1994 pre-season friendly against Raith
    Rovers, in which one ended up with a broken nose and
    was carried away on a stretcher, and the pair received a
    14-match and a 10-match ban?

11 Which player was fined a maximum of two weeks'
    wages by Hearts in 2009 for 'unacceptable conduct'?
    The player in question had launched a tirade against
    the manager in front of his teammates, criticising his
    tactics during a match in which he had not even played –
    because he had already been exiled from the first team.

A Mixed Bag

No quiz worth its salt would be complete without a general knowledge round, so here it is – a section without a particular theme; just an assortment of questions about Hearts on no particular topic.

1 Who were Hearts' first shirt sponsors?

2 Which golfer, while leading the Open Championship at the halfway stage, confessed that because he couldn't play much golf during the winter due to crippling arthritis, it was going to Tynecastle every other Saturday to watch Hearts that stopped him from 'going insane'?

3 Kevin Keegan played for Hearts in a testimonial match at Tynecastle. Whose testimonial was it?

4 Who was the first player to be inducted into the Hearts Hall of Fame in 2006?

5 In November 1996, at an Edinburgh derby match, Hearts mascot 'Hearty Harry' performed his usual half-time routine, cavorting with young fans, before removing the head of his mascot suit to reveal himself as which famous personality?

6 Which Hearts player's uncle became his country's first-ever Olympic champion when he won the 400m hurdles in a world-record time during the 1972 Games in Munich?

7 Who are the only two Hearts players to have been named as the Scottish Football Writers' Footballer of the Year?

8   Which was the first Hearts match to be shown live
    on television?

9   What was the venue for the Hearts v. Rangers Scottish
    Youth Cup final in May 2014?

10 Which German club came to Tynecastle to play a friendly
    match and help cash-strapped Hearts raise funds during
    the 2013–14 season?

11 Why did Hearts turn down an invitation by UEFA to
    play in the inaugural European Cup and become the first
    Scottish club to do so?

The Romanov Years

1 John Robertson.

2 He swam across Loch Ness.

3 Fourteen (John Robertson, George Burley, John McGlynn, Steven Pressley, Graham Rix, Valdas Ivanauskas, Eduard Malofeev, Egenijus Riabovas, Anatoly Korobochka, Steven Frail, Csaba Laszlo, Jim Jefferies, Paulo Sergio, Gary Locke).

4 Phil Anderton. He was the Hearts chief executive appointed in 2005, who, while holding the equivalent position at the Scottish Rugby Union, laid on lavish fireworks displays before rugby internationals at Murrayfield. England coach Sir Clive Woodward criticised the display, saying it was 'more like a pop concert than a rugby match' after the 2004 Calcutta Cup.

5 The Scottish football media.

6 Roman Bednar.

7 Siroki Brijeg of Bosnia in 2006.

8 Steven Pressley, Craig Gordon and Paul Hartley, who called a press conference to complain publicly about the way in which Vladimir Romanov was running the club. The Tynecastle careers of Pressley and Hartley were short-lived thereafter.

9 Dundee United.

10 He worked as a painter and decorator.

11 Ukio Bankas.

In the Beginning

1 Mother Anderson's Tavern on West Crosscauseway.
2 The 3rd Edinburgh Rifle Volunteers.
3 All white.
4 The Edinburgh FA Cup of 1878. Hearts beat Hibs 3–2 at Powburn in the fourth replay of the final after 4 draws.
5 Dalry Primrose.
6 Aston Villa (lost 2–4), Blackburn Rovers (lost 0–2).
7 21–0 against Anchor FC.
8 The club was found guilty of professionalism. Two players were found to have been paid 26s per week, at a time when paying players was illegal.
9 Rangers at Old Ibrox. Hearts were defeated 5–2.
10 1894–95.
11 Portsmouth.

Goals, Goals, Goals

1 Jimmy Murray, who scored in a 1–1 draw with Yugoslavia in the 1958 World Cup finals.

2 Morton. Hearts won 3–2 at Cappielow after being 2–0 down.

3 Tommy Murray, in a 1–0 victory in December 1972.

4 Bobby Walker, who played from Hearts from 1896 to 1919.

5 7.

6 Scott Robinson (*vs.* Ross County).

7 Allan Johnston.

8 Justin Fashanu (Hearts, 1993–94) who won the 1980 award for a spectacular goal for Norwich City against Liverpool.

9 Kilmarnock were defeated 8–2. Hearts scorers were Donald Ford (5), Danny Ferguson (2), Eddie O'Donnell.

10 Ryan Stevenson (winner against Hibs in the League Cup) .

11 Steven Pressley (penalty) and Mark de Vries.

Round 4

Hearts in Europe

1 Ian Crawford (*vs.* Standard Liege in the European Cup in 1958).
2 Bordeaux.
3 Mark de Vries (Hearts beat Bordeaux 1–0, but eventually lost the tie 2–1 on aggregate).
4 FC Lausanne-Sport (Inter-Cities Fairs Cup, 1963).
5 Estadio Lluis Sitjar (*vs.* Real Mallorca, 1998). They only agreed to continue after the bizarre sight of a tractor arriving on the pitch to remove some turf, dig out the undersoil and replace the turf was witnessed – a plan which was aborted at the last moment.
6 Roy Kay.
7 Alan Gordon (*vs.* Inter Milan, Inter-Cities Fairs Cup, 1961).
8 After drawing 3–3 and 2–2 (away goals did not count double at that time), Hearts lost the toss to host the third match decider, and went down 1–0 in Zaragoza.
9 Videoton.
10 Dennis Wyness.
11 Pepe Reina.

1 His son, William McCartney.
2 Bobby Moncur (for Newcastle United against Ujpesti Dozsa in the 1969 Inter Cities Fairs Cup final, won 6–2 on aggregate).
3 Graham Rix (Arsenal *v.* Valencia, 1980 European Cup Winners' Cup final).
4 George Burley.
5 Joe Jordan.
6 He had been a First Division referee.
7 Eduard Malofeev (23 October to 20 November 2006).
8 Future Hearts manager Csaba Laszlo, then of Ferencvaros.
9 Eamonn Bannon.
10 Willie Ormond (Hearts were in the First Division at the time).
11 Csaba Laszlo (season 2008–09; he also won the SPL's equivalent award that year).

Hearts Against the 'Wee Team'

1. 4 (out of 5).
2. George Hogg.
3. Edgaras Jankauskas.
4. Christian Nade, Gary Glen.
5. Hearts 1 Hibs 0. The match was played in the East Meadows in 1875. Hearts played with only eight men for the first 20 minutes.
6. Phil Stamp.
7. Black Sabbath.
8. It was the first match in the famous sequence of 22 games in a row without losing to Hibs.
9. Gary McSwegan.
10. John Collins.
11. 27 goals.

1 Steven Pressley.
2 Jim Townsend, Alan Anderson and Jim Cruickshank.
3 Freddie Warren, who played for Hearts from 1936 until the outbreak of the Second World War in 1939.
4 Goalkeeper Jack Harkness, who won a further 9 caps while at Tynecastle.
5 Tom Jenkinson, who played in a 4–1 victory over Northern Ireland in February 1887.
6 Tommy Walker (9 goals).
7 Kevin McKenna (7 goals for Canada); Saulius Mikoliunas (25 caps for Lithuania).
8 He scored in a 1–0 away victory over Bulgaria. The win enabled the Republic of Ireland to finish top of Group 7, 1 point ahead of Bulgaria, thus qualifying for the European Championships of 1988 – the first time they had ever reached a major finals. Gary has been a national hero in Ireland ever since.
9 Harry Rennie, a former half-back, who made his debut in 1900 as Scotland beat England 4–1 at Celtic Park.
10 Takis Fyssas (Greece, who won Euro 2004).
11 Craig Levein (Hearts 2000–2004, Scotland 2009–2012); Eduard Malofeev (Soviet Union 1984–86, Hearts 2006); Willie Ormond (Scotland 1973–77, Hearts 1977–1980).

Keep it in the Family

1 Tommy White (his brother John was a member of Tottenham Hotspur's double-winning team of 1960–61).

2 Gordon Marshall. (Hearts goalkeeper of the late 1950s and early 1960s, whose son, also Gordon, followed in his footsteps between the sticks.)

3 Jamie Walker. (Grandad Tommy Walker was the legendary manager of the Hearts team which won two League titles, a Scottish Cup and four League Cups in the 1950s and '60s.)

4 Justin Fashanu. (Brother John played for Norwich City, Millwall, Aston Villa and Wimbledon, with whom he won the FA Cup in 1988.)

5 Lee Johnson (father Gary played for Watford and several Swedish clubs before managing Cambridge United, Kettering, Latvia, Yeovil Town twice, Bristol City, Peterborough United and Northampton Town).

6 Kevin Hegarty. (Brother Paul also captained Dundee United in the 1987 UEFA Cup final.)

7 Colin McAdam, who played 6 times for Hearts in 1985 and 1986. Rangers had converted him to striker, and he played directly opposite his brother Tom, a Celtic defender.

8 Darren Beckford. (Brother Jason came up through Manchester City junior ranks while Darren was playing for their first team.)

9 Andy Bowman (played in the League Championship-winning teams of 1957–58 and 1959–60; son Dave made 156 competitive appearances for Hearts between 1980 and 1984).

10 Fabien Leclercq. (Brother-in-law Stephane Adam scored the deciding goal in the 2–1 victory over Rangers in the 1998 Scottish Cup final, ending thirty-six years without winning a trophy.)
11 Ian Black (played for Hearts 1978–80). Ian Jr followed him into the Hearts team.

Scottish Cup Glory

1 Willie Fernie.
2 Only 1, when they beat Celtic 3–1 in the final.
3 Third Lanark were beaten 1–0. Hearts wore light blue.
4 Steven Pressley, Robbie Neilson, Rudi Skacel and Michal Pospisil.
5 Valdas Ivanauskas.
6 Isaac Begbie.
7 Hearts goalkeeper Gilles Rousset.
8 Willie Young.
9 Logie Green in Edinburgh, which was the home ground of St Bernards.
10 Ibrox Park.
11 Jamie Hamill.

The Legends

1 Dave Mackay (won Footballer of the Year jointly with Tony Book in 1969).
2 Larissa (in Greece).
3 Czechoslovakia, West Germany, Wales.
4 USA.
5 John Cumming, who won seven medals having played in all seven League Championship, Scottish Cup and League Cup-winning teams during the golden period between 1954 and 1962.
6 Jim Jefferies who, of course, also served two spells as Hearts manager and ended the club's thirty-six-year trophy drought when he guided the team to Scottish Cup success in 1998.
7 Hearts were in war-torn Mostar in Bosnia, where they played Velez Mostar, en route to the fourth round of the UEFA Cup.
8 King Haakon of Norway. It was a match against Kristiana Kredlag, during Hearts' first foreign tour.
9 Dave Mackay, Tommy Walker, Willie Bauld and Alex Young.
10 Joe Davis.
11 Alex Young. After winning two Scottish League Championships, one Scottish Cup and a Scottish League Cup with Hearts, he added an English League Championship and FA Cup for Everton, who dubbed him 'The Golden Vision'. Celebrated filmmaker Ken Loach used the nickname as the title of a BBC documentary about Young.

Home is Where the Hearts Are

1 The East Meadows, which was a communal ground used by several teams.
2 Archibald Leitch; Sheffield Wednesday.
3 Powderhall.
4 Rapid Vienna, who were beaten 5–1 in an exhibition match in 1934.
5 Sunderland.
6 Bolton Wanderers, who were duly beaten 4–1.
7 FC Braga of Portugal. Hearts won 3–1.
8 The club badge, painted over the entrance to the players' tunnel.
9 Franz Beckenbauer (Hearts 1 Bayern Munich 0, 28 February 1989).
10 Nine times.
11 Scotland v. Samoa (the Samoans won 20–12).

Hearts Against the Auld Enemy

1 Manchester City.
2 Manchester United.
3 Alan Curbishley.
4 Ralph Callachan.
5 The first leg, played in London, finished 0–0. The second leg was played in Edinburgh in January 1902, with Hearts winning 3–1.
6 It was one of the matches played in Sir Stanley Matthews' Farewell Tour (Stoke won 2–1).
7 Darwen FC, who beat Hearts 7–1 in October 1886. The Scottish Football Association subsequently banned its members from playing in this 'Sassenach' competition.
8 Brighton and Hove Albion. The match finished 2–2, John Robertson having scored both Hearts goals. Brighton won 4–2 in a penalty shoot-out.
9 George Fleming.
10 Burnley.
11 Spanish youngster Juanjo scored the winner. Stan Collymore was making his Fulham debut.

Aye, Aye Cap'n

1　Jake Reid.
2　Dave Mackay (having enjoyed no little success with Tottenham Hotspur and Derby County in between!).
3　Eddie Thomson.
4　Bobby Parker.
5　Robbie Neilson.
6　Alex Massie.
7　Colin Cameron (signed from Raith Rovers).
8　Michael Stewart.
9　Gary Locke.
10　They were both lining up against their former clubs.
　　Hearts captain George Miller was an ex-Dunfermline player.
　　His opposite number, Roy Barry, had played for Hearts.
11　Christophe Berra.

Just Champion

1   Jimmy Wardhaugh, who scored both goals in a 2–1 home win over Rangers, the final League match of the season.

2   Third Lanark, who held Hearts to a goalless draw at Cathkin Park.

3   A 3–2 away win against St Mirren secured the title with 2 matches still to go. Aberdeen and Rangers were still to be beaten, 4–0 and 2–1 respectively.

4   Hearts lost 2–1 away to Clyde.

5   13 points. (Hearts finished on 62 points, Rangers were second on 49 – a remarkably emphatic achievement in the days when only 2 points were awarded for a win.)

6   Alex Young, with 23 League goals (28 in all competitions that season).

7   St Mirren again – a 4–4 draw at Love Street.

8   They won their first 11 League fixtures.

9   Clyde (twice). The only other point dropped during the season was in a goalless draw at home to Rangers.

10 Gordon Smith, who – having already won a League title with Hibs – would become the only player to do so with three different clubs (he later won a Championship medal with Dundee) – and not one of them was Rangers or Celtic!

11 Hibernian.

Get a Move On

1 Reuben Palazuelos (signed from Gimnastica in Spain).
2 Denis Prychynenko, who took German citizenship and ceased being Ukrainian, to avoid needing an EU work permit.
3 Willie Pettigrew and Derek Addison (who had both been signed from Dundee United).
4 Allan Johnston, who moved to Rennes in France.
5 Arthur Mann, who was sold to Manchester City for £65,000.
6 Shandong Luneng Taishan.
7 Andy Webster, who signed for Wigan Athletic.
   The landmark case became known as the 'Webster ruling'. FIFA subsequently ruled that he had cancelled his contract with Hearts 'without just cause', suspended him for 2 matches and ordered him to pay Hearts compensation of £625,000 (the amount was later reduced to £150,000).
8 Neil MacFarlane (he moved to Aberdeen during the January transfer window that season).
9 It was part of a dispute over an incentive bonus for winning promotion back to the Premier League at the first attempt. Following a board meeting, the directors decided to make most of the players available for sale.
10 Full-back George Thomson.
11 Full-back Hugh Burns.

Jambograms

1   Thomas Flogel. The Vienna-born favourite was a member of the Hearts team which defeated Rangers 2–1 in the 1998 Scottish Cup final.

2   Gordon Smith, the silky skilled winger who played in the Hearts team that beat Third Lanark in the Scottish League Cup final in his first season with the club (1959–60) and ended it by collecting a Scottish League Championship medal as well.

3   Willie Duff. Goalkeeper in the 1956 Scottish Cup-winning team. Also won the Scottish League Cup in 1954.

4   Takis Fyssas. Left wing-back who played in the 2006 Scottish Cup-winning team.

5   Danny Grainger, who scored with a penalty in the 5–1 demolition of Hibs in the 2012 Scottish Cup final.

6   George Thomson, who won two Scottish League Championships and two Scottish League Cups with Hearts before being transferred to Everton in 1960.

7   Davie Baird, who won three Scottish Cups with Hearts – in 1891, 1896 and 1901 (the only Hearts player to have done so).

8   Norrie Davidson, scorer of the winning goal in the 1962 Scottish League Cup final.

9   Ibrahim Tall – played in the 2006 Scottish Cup-winning team.

10 Ryan McGowan, scorer against Hibs in the 2012 Scottish Cup final victory, and subsequently left to play football in China.

11 Goalkeeper Gilles Rousset, who starred in the 1998 Scottish Cup final victory over Rangers having been on the end of a 5–1 reverse at the hands of the same opponents two years earlier.

As Low as it Gets

1 A 2–2 draw away to Kilmarnock was not enough to save Hearts, who were officially relegated the following day when Motherwell defeated Dundee United 4-0.

2 Ten defeats in a row. Hearts, who finished second bottom, were 11 points below eighth-placed Partick Thistle.

3 0.042 of a goal. At that time, goal average rather than goal difference was taken into account and Hearts lost out, having scored 90 goals over the course of the season compared with Kilmarnock's 62.

4 Partick Thistle.

5 Alan Gordon.

6 6.

7 Roddy McDonald.

8 Cala Homes, £20.5 million. The crisis was averted when Vladimir Romanov bought a controlling interest in the debt-ridden club. Robinson's document: 'Tynecastle: Not Fit For Purpose' was later exposed as a web of lies.

9 15 points.

10 Gordon Durie, who scored in Rangers' 5–1 victory.

11 St Mirren (Hearts won 1–0).

1 Queen of the South.
2 Mo Berthe.
3 Derek O'Connor.
4 Drew Young.
5 Andy Thorn from Wimbledon.
6 Gary Naysmith.
7 Gilles Rousset.
8 FC Dordrecht of the Netherlands.
9 Number 21.
10 Tommy Murray.
11 Jeremy Goss, signed from Norwich City,
    who had won 9 caps for Wales.

The Terrible Trio

1. Jimmy Wardhaugh – who was born at Marshall Meadows, just over the border in England.
2. Austria, at Hampden in 1956 (he scored Scotland's goal in a 1–1 draw).
3. Sunderland.
4. Davie McLean.
5. East Fife. Hearts, bottom of the League at the time, won 6–1, with Bauld claiming a hat-trick and Conn scoring twice.
6. The RAF.
7. They worked down the pits as 'Bevin Boys'.
8. 'Twinkletoes'.
9. Cristiano Ronaldo.
10. Johannesburg Ramblers.
11. Jimmy Wardhaugh.

1 They won their first 8 matches.
2 Sixteen.
3 The Usher Hall.
4 'C' Company of the 16th Royal Scots, though they were familiarly known as McCrae's Battalion (sometimes known as 'The Footballers' Battalion').
5 4 points (and 11 ahead of third-placed Rangers).
6 Contalmaison.
7 Manager of the Tivoli picture house in Gorgie Road.
8 *The Hearts and the Great War.*
9 Seven – James Speedie, John Allan, Duncan Currie, James Boyd, Ernie Ellis and Harry Wattie were killed in action. Tom Gracie, having also served in the trenches, took ill and died in hospital of leukaemia. Among those wounded in action were Jamie Low, Annan Ness, Alfie Briggs, Paddy Crossan, Ernie McGuire, Bob Mercer, John Wilson, Willie Wilson, Robert Preston, John Martin, George Miller, Neil Moreland, George Sinclair and James Hazeldean.
10 Bob Mercer.
11 Robert Munro, Secretary of State for Scotland.

1 Harry Kane.
2 He joined the police force.
3 Jock Fairbairn (1890–98).
4 Cowdenbeath.
5 Eduardas Kurskis.
6 Henry Smith (214 clean sheets in 701 appearances).
   He was signed by Tony Ford.
7 Marian Kello.
8 Kenny Garland.
9 French.
10 Gordon Marshall.
11 Antti Niemi who played for Southampton against Arsenal
   in 2003 and Peter Enckelman who played for Cardiff City
   against Portsmouth in 2008.

The Greatest Game in History

1 Jamie McDonald, Ryan McGowan, Andy Webster, Marius Zaliukas, Danny Grainger, Suso Santana, Ian Black, Darren Barr, Rudi Skacel, Andrew Driver, Stephen Elliott.

2 14 minutes.

3 Craig Thomson.

4 Andy Webster (Dundee United), Darren Barr (Falkirk).

5 Darren Barr, Rudi Skacel (2), Danny Grainger (pen), Ryan McGowan.

6 Suso Santana, Rudi Skacel, Ian Black, Stephen Elliott.

7 Suso Santana.

8 He made an obscene gesture to the Hearts fans.

9 Rudi Skacel.

10 Craig Beattie, Mehdi Taouil, Scott Robinson.

11 Romanian club CFR Cluj.

The World at Our Feet

1 Saulius Mikoliunas (made his debut on 25 January 2005).
2 Roald Jensen, the very popular Norwegian winger, who made his first appearance in January 1965.
3 Marius Zaliukas (222 appearances up to June 2013).
4 Rudi Skacel (48 goals).
5 Samuel Camazzola (Brazil), Fernando Screpis (Argentina) and Mauricio Pinilla (Chile).
6 Edgaras Jankauskas, who won the Champions League with FC Porto.
7 Fiorentina.
8 South Africa, where he won the League title with Kaizer Chiefs.
9 Jose Quitongo (Angola).
10 Wilfred Ouefio.
11 George Wright.

1 Forfar Athletic.
2 Gordon Smith.
3 Juho Makela.
4 George Fleming.
5 Muirton Park, Perth.
6 Danny Grainger, Rudi Skacel.
7 Brechin City.
8 Gary Mackay scored 4 times in a 6–0 win.
9 Huntly, 6–0 (yes, same score again!)
10 Starks Park, Kirkcaldy. Fabien Leclercq made his debut.
11 Andrius Velicka.

The Scottish League Cup

1. Willie Bauld (70 goals in 76 appearances).
2. Marius Zaliukas, who scored twice in the 3–1 win over Livingston in the third round.
3. After losing the League Championship on goal average in 1965, Hearts led the campaign for goal difference to be used instead. Having finished level on points with Morton at the end of the group stage of the League Cup in 1969, they became the first club to lose out by means of goal difference.
4. Motherwell were beaten 4–2 in the 1954 final.
5. Neil McCann.
6. Willie Bauld (Hearts 4 Motherwell 2).
7. Alex Young, in the 2–1 victory over Third Lanark.
8. The match was played at Celtic Park because Hampden Park was being rebuilt.
9. Hearts' John Sutton, who had formerly played for St Mirren.
10. Dundee, at Dens Park.
11. Andrius Velicka.

Loan Stars

1 Tivoli Gardens (Jamaica).
2 Danny Wilson from Liverpool.
3 Kieran McAnespie, who played for Hearts on loan from Fulham in 2000–01.
4 Gregor Stevens, who joined on loan from Rangers in 1983–84.
5 Queen of the South (for whom he played in the 2008 Scottish Cup final).
6 Andy Tod, who played 3 matches for Hearts in 2002.
7 Hartlepool United.
8 Robbie Neilson.
9 Paul McCallum.
10 Tepi Moilanen.
11 Kevin McHattie.

Never Go Back

1 Dave McPherson, who also had two spells at Rangers (but won the majority of his caps while at Hearts).
2 Donald Park (played for Partick Thistle between his two spells at Tynecastle).
3 Rudi Skacel.
4 Michael Stewart (returned as a permanent signing two years later and was subsequently appointed as club captain by manager Csaba Laszlo).
5 Ryan Stevenson, who moved from Hearts to Ipswich Town in January 2012 and returned to Tynecastle just seven months later.
6 Willie Hamilton (who also played for Edinburgh's 'wee team').
7 Neil McCann (Man of the Match in League Cup final against Rangers in 1996; scored on debut for Falkirk against Hearts in 2008).
8 John Colquhoun.
9 Alan Gordon.
10 Eamonn Bannon.
11 John Robertson ('The Hammer of the Hibs').

The Record Breakers

1 Bobby Parker (357 times as captain).

2 Steven Pressley, who won 32 caps while he was at Tynecastle.

3 Mirsad Beslija, who was bought from Racing Genk of Belgium for a fee of £850,000.

4 Barney Battles scored 44 League goals in season 1930–31.

5 It was against Hibs, in a 2–1 defeat at Easter Road in April 1998.

6 Scott Robinson, who was 16 years, 1 month and 14 days old when he played against Inverness Caledonian Thistle in April 2008.

7 Hearts 10 Hibs 2, on 12 August 1893.

8 Gary Mackay, who holds the record for the highest number of Hearts appearances. A lifelong Hearts fan, he was reputed to spend so much time at Tynecastle, it was suggested he should be given the keys to lock up every night – hence the nickname.

9 Former captain Marius Zaliukas, who was red-carded seven times.

10 1931–32. (53,396 watched Hearts v. Rangers on 13 February 1932.)

11 Scottish Cup semi-final against Motherwell at Hampden on 29 March 1952.

Bad Boys

1   Andy Davis.
2   Dougie McDonald.
3   Derek Adams of Ross County.
4   Stephane Paille.
5   Pasquale Bruno, David Weir, Paul Ritchie and Neil Pointon.
6   He was wearing an earring.
7   He forced them to run up and down the steps in the
    Tynecastle stands carrying full bags of golf clubs, then
    ordered them to bring their clubs to training every day
    for a week and carry them as they slogged round the
    running track.
8   Michael Stewart, Ismael Bouzid, Ian Black and Suso Santana.
    (Stewart later had his red card downgraded to a caution).
9   For bouncing the ball off Aberdeen player John Hewitt's face.
10 Craig Levein and Graeme Hogg.
11 Laryea Kingston, whose tirade came after a 2–2 draw with
    St Johnstone. He had previously aroused manager Csaba
    Laszlo's anger after he reported for duty with Ghana
    despite being on Hearts' injury list. He had not played
    for the club since the start of the season, then played in
    2 international matches and insisted his loyalty lay with his
    country rather than his club.

A Mixed Bag

1 Alexanders of Edinburgh.

2 Andrew Oldcorn (although some would say
   that regular visits to Tynecastle has the opposite effect!).

3 Alex MacDonald.

4 Dave Mackay.

5 Rangers striker Ally McCoist, who had come to Tynecastle
   just to watch the match between Hearts and Hibs, but
   ended up inside the Hearty Harry costume for a laugh, just
   a week before he was due to play against Hearts in the
   Scottish League Cup final.

6 David Obua. His uncle was John Akii-Bua of Uganda.

7 Sandy Jardine (1985–86) and Craig Gordon (2005–06).

8 Hearts v. Standard Liege, European Cup, September 1958.
   Hearts won 2–1 but lost the tie 6–3 on aggregate.

9 St Mirren Park.

10 Wolfsburg.

11 Foreign travel was rare and more complicated in those days
    and the club had been warned that they would face a points
    deduction if they did not return from a European fixture in
    time to fulfil their next League match. Chelsea also declined
    after a similarly strong warning by the English FA. Participants
    were not necessarily their national League champions, but
    were chosen by the French football magazine *L'Equipe*, having
    been deemed to be the sixteen most prestigious clubs in
    Europe. After Hearts declined, Hibernian were invited as an
    acceptable alternative and reached the semi-finals.

Bibliography

All the questions in this book have been devised by myself, based on a lifetime of following Heart of Midlothian Football Club and on a comprehensive knowledge of the history of the club. The majority of the answers are derived from my own memory of the events, matches, players and other personnel, having witnessed them myself.

However, in the interests of accuracy and proper research, I have also used a few other sources to corroborate the answers by checking dates, results, goalscorers, name spellings, etc. in order to counter any tricks of the memory caused by the ageing process!

As always in any quiz worth its salt, however, the questionmaster's answer is always final!

I am indebted to the following publications and other sources which have occasionally been used for reference:

Alexander, Jack, *McCrae's Battalion: The Story of the 16th Royal Scots* (Mainstream Publishing, 2003). This is the definitive book on the great Hearts team that volunteered en masse for active service during the First World War. Every Hearts fan should have a copy of this book on their bookshelf.

Speed, David, Bill Smith and Graham Blackwood, *The Heart of Midlothian Football Club: A Pictorial History 1874–1984* (Heart of Midlothian FC, 1984)

Price, Norrie, *Gritty, Gallant, Glorious: A History and Complete Record of the Hearts 1946–1997* (Norrie Price, 1997)

The Scotsman

The London Hearts Supporters Club website (www.londonhearts.com)

Also from The History Press

BACK OF THE NET!